# YES, I'VE MADE MISTAKES

## YOUR PAST DOESN'T HAVE
## TO DETERMINE YOUR FUTURE

How to reposition your life for success after
a setback caused by bad decisions

## By Daroun Maurice Jamison

*Yes I've Made Mistakes: Your Past Doesn't Have to Determine Your Future*
Second Edition

For information or to order copies, contact Daroun Jamison at www.cafedaroun.com.

First Edition, 2014

Manufactured in USA

Daroun Jamison is a remarkable example of personal transformation and self-empowerment. He brings a hard earned message of **self-empowerment through self-examination and personal responsibility**, a message that asserts that each of us has the capacity to be better and do better. A clear message about the power of humanity.

Raised by a single mother in the housing projects in Wilmington, Delaware, Daroun struggled with self-esteem, bullies and identity issues. In 1995 at the age of 17, he was incarcerated and received an 18-year sentence for gun violence.

Barely able to read, angry and confused, he resolved that he wanted better for himself than to die in prison. After being denied access to a treatment program, he began educating himself. Through a combination of reading, meditation and self-examination he was able to transcend the mindset that nearly destroyed his life.

His story is one of hope, resilience and faith that resonates and inspires. He has the ability to cut across racial, cultural and social economic barriers to connect with people from all walks of life with a clear message about the power of humanity.

He is currently enrolled in community college, working on up and coming projects and launching the D. Maurice Education Group L.L.C to help enrich and empower lives using the lessons that have enriched and empowered his own life.

Learn more about Daroun at www.cafedaroun.com.

# Dedication

## To My Father
## Mr. Elee Kennedy, Jr.
### May 18, 1938 to December 9, 2014

*I put on a brave face in public, but the truth is that I can't stop crying.*

*I find myself having to make an effort not to, but the truth is that I can't stop crying,*

*I fight the tears at work and sometimes go into the bathroom, but I can't stop crying,*

*I cry when I am home. I cry when I am alone. I cry when I write. I am crying right now.*

*My mother says that I am your legacy, and I am. My heart is heavy, and I can't explain what this pain is like. I wanted you to see me in this moment. I wanted you to see this moment.*

*I am beyond grateful for the three years we shared and that we were able to rebuild our relationship and prove that damaged relationships between fathers and sons can be repaired. That wounds can be healed. But I still can't stop crying.*

# Special Acknowledgement

Mrs. Christine O'Brien... Yes, Chris, you get your very own page.

This book is possible because of your support, love and confidence in me, my writing and what I seek to accomplish. Thank you for reading my material, editing and helping me become a better writer.

You and Bob have become an unexpected blessing in my life as friends, mentors, guides and family. If not for your gentle persistence and Dr. Yasser Payne's encouragement it's unlikely that I would have enrolled in college.

Words alone cannot express my appreciation for all of your support. I imagine that the only authentic way for me to show it is by continuing to become a better human being and working hard to add value to the lives of our young people.

# Additional Acknowledgements

It takes a village to develop a leader.

While it is true that self-determination and willpower have brought me a long way in my journey to this point, it is equally true that *faith* has played and even greater role— *faith* that I could succeed even when there was no evidence to support it. I just knew that I would not be guided to a river without there being a way to cross it.

That river symbolizes my reintegration into society and my efforts to build an education company that will enrich the lives of our youth and young adults and add value to the community. I heard the calling deep in my spirit and I obeyed.

In my obedience I arrived at the river with determination but no idea how I would get across. I stood looking at the challenge and lowered my head in deep thought, meditation and prayer. I was reminding myself that I am here for a reason. When I raised my head, my angels had arrived.

With gratitude I would like to acknowledge those who have believed in and supported me in my efforts to use my life experience to help to improve the lives of others:

The Jamison; Kennedy; Whalen; Carter; Pinkney and Bowden Families; Deacon and Mrs. James Bonds; Dr. Christopher Alan Bullock, senior minister/pastor at Canaan Baptist Church, New Castle, Delaware; Robert and Christine O'Brien; Ms. Emlyn DeGannes; Ms. Rose Wooten; Dr. Yasser Payne; Ken Anderson; Marsha Carter; Danny 'ACE' Valentine; Kenny Williams; Rochele Barham; Matt and Lauren Swift; Brenne Shepperson; Ashley Biden; Tyrone Bryant; Haneef Salaam; Zaki Muslim; Cameron and Yana Jones; Rebecca Johnson; Tamara N. Varella; John Childress; Greg Reaves; Darnyelle Jervey; Michael Kalmback; Michael Pipkins; Michael Harris; Geronimo Vannicola; Joshua Hilton; Nugi Nicoles; Coley Harris; Judy Cohen; Nancy Linwood Lewis; DESSA Toastmasters; Eugena Roache; M. Rivera; Diane Barnes; and anyone else who can call me and ask why I didn't mention them.

*"Success is to be measured not so much by the position that one has reached in life as by the obstacles which he has overcome".*

**Booker T. Washington**

# Contents

Introduction ........................................................ 12

1    My Journey Here: The Back Story .............. 14

2    Choosing to Do Better ................................ 28

3    How Did I Get into This Mess? .................... 35

4    Mindset, Decisions and Outcomes (MDO) . 39

5    Mistakes and Bad Decisions ....................... 45

6    A Foundation for Change ............................ 52

7    Preparing for Change ................................. 67

8    Keys to Success .......................................... 70

9    The Challenges Ahead ................................ 83

10   What It Means to Be Human ...................... 87

# Introduction

Life is a continuous cycle of *mindset, decisions* and *outcomes*. I call it the **M.D.O. Cycle**, and it begins with a want, desire or need for something that has value to you. From basic survival needs to recreational pleasures we are continuously making decisions that we hope will either bring us pleasure or help us to avoid pain.

We make our decisions based on our mindsets or beliefs about how to get the things we want out of life. These beliefs are not always correct and may lead to bad experiences. The result is that we sometimes make decisions that get us everything *except* what we want. So instead of solving our problem, we end up creating more problems for ourselves.

Life in its core is a process of growth and development. We all have ups and downs. If during the low points of our lives we are unable to pick ourselves up and move forward, we can't accomplish our goals. Our setbacks can become barriers to our happiness and success because their weight will hold us down

This is a book intent on addressing one central question: How do we move forward with our lives after experiencing a personal setback caused by bad decisions? It is based on real life experience and offers practical and thought-provoking advice to help you to reposition your life after a personal setback. It aims to inspire and empower you with strategies to help improve your decision making skills and to overcome bad decisions.

This book is for you or someone you care about if:

- You or they have faced a difficult period in life and as a result made a bad decision that has made life more complicated.

- You or they are trying to be better and do better but are having a hard time getting back on track.

- You or they are looking for real life solutions.

# 1    My Journey Here: The Back Story

I am in the most basic and fundamental sense a traveler on this road of life just like you are. The road isn't always easy, and none of us were born with instructions on how to succeed, be happy and at peace within ourselves. During the journey we try to figure out who we are, why we are here, what is our purpose and what are we going to do with our lives.

Along the way we have experiences, some good and others not so good, that teach us lessons about life. At some point most of us are called to share those lessons with fellow travelers to help them along their way to finding peace, happiness and success. Those fellow travelers may be children or adults, family members, friends, mentees or complete strangers.

I wrote this book to share some of the lessons that I have learned about life while on my own journey. My journey has been a struggle, filled with bad decisions and setbacks.

There were times when the challenges I faced seemed so hard and hopeless that I considered suicide and couldn't imagine my life getting any better.

My views and advice are based on personal experience. I speak what I know and teach what I strive really hard to live. Although imperfect and subject to error like everyone else, I am in essence who I say that I am.

In what was perhaps the darkest period of my life I sat in a prison cell struggling to imagine the possibility that I could rebuild my life. I had almost destroyed myself through a series of reckless and bad decisions. These decisions reflected a mindset or way of thinking that could only produce negativity in my life, but I didn't understand any of that back then.

## Summer 1995

Twenty years ago, I was approaching my eighteenth birthday with more issues than I knew how to handle. It was the summer of 1995, and I was out of control and homeless. In a few short years I had gone from a church-going kid to full-blown thug with no respect for myself, my elders or community. To say that I lost my way would be an understatement because I had also lost myself in trying to be someone that I wasn't.

My family had been evicted from our home in the public housing projects of Wilmington, Delaware, and my mother and two younger siblings were staying in a shelter. For the second time in my life I reached my boiling point and decided I had to take action. I wanted better for myself than the constant uncertainty of when and if I would eat or where I would sleep. I was determined to do something to improve the conditions of my life.

A few years prior I had reached my first boiling point as a result of being constantly bullied. I had decided then that enough was enough. I wanted better for myself than living in constant fear, being picked on, devalued and beaten up. And this is where everything started falling apart.

To say that my issues from being bullied were devastating would be a gross understatement. Almost every aspect of my childhood was impacted. More than anything my self-image and esteem were damaged almost beyond repair.

As a quiet church kid with deeply stained front teeth, I seemed to welcome my tormentors into my life. And torment me they did, with exceptional skills. I had no idea how to handle it. Although I grew up in an aggressive and violent environment, I was not by nature aggressive nor violent.

I became so lost in the constant fear of being humiliated on the school bus and in class that I started to hate myself. I just couldn't understand what I was doing wrong to anyone besides breathing. In high school my grades were horrible and my behavior was even worse.

I was not only failing all of my classes but getting suspended quiet often for fighting. Having reached my boiling point, I became aggressive, violent and out of control. Drugs and crime soon followed. I couldn't see that my life was spiraling out of control or that I was losing myself and becoming someone that my mother couldn't recognize. All I saw was that I was no longer being bullied and picked on and that my behavior was an acceptable way to resolve conflict and solve problems.

So in 1995, when I was homeless, hungry and extremely frustrated, I woke up one morning determined to do something about my situation.

I didn't wake up that morning with the intent or desire to hurt anyone. I woke up that morning determined to survive and succeed. I woke up that morning thinking that enough is enough and something was going to change. And that was the day that everything in my life changed.

By the end of the night not only had I failed in improving conditions, I had made them far worse and more complicated than ever before. I recall hiding in a tree that night by some railroad tracks in South Wilmington, trying to figure out my next steps as the cops searched the city for me.

The following night I turned myself in and sat in a holding cell at the Wilmington police station contemplating my fate. A young man, whom I had shot accidentally, was in the hospital fighting for his life, and I was assured that murder charges were coming.

I didn't know how to feel about anything. I certainly didn't mean to shoot him; I was trying to shoot someone else.

I was afraid to feel bad because to do so, I imagined, would plunge me back into the weak guy that was bullied and mistreated. My solution was to just push my actions into the deepest corner of my mind and not think about them.

I was very fortunate that my victim survived and thankful that I didn't have murder to add to my conscience. I was charged with two counts of attempted murder, multiple gun charges, assault and conspiracy I believe. A year later I accepted a plea agreement to an eighteen-year prison sentence. I would sit in prison from age 17 in 1995 until 2011 when I was 34.

## Sixteen Years in a Prison Cell

I was still 18 when I accepted the plea agreement and couldn't imagine what life would look like for me when my sentence was over. I was angry, depressed and struggling to picture being able to rebuild my life after prison.

I wanted to know where it all went wrong and if it was even possible for me to succeed. I couldn't understand what had happened to my life. How did I go from a junior deacon being groomed to become a minister, with dreams of joining the air force, into a violent, drug-dealing high school dropout with aspirations of becoming a gangster rapper who died before the age of 23?

Over and over I asked myself, would my past determine my future? Was I destined to return to the streets and prison? Or could I make a comeback and not only be successful, but also be the type of man that my family and community could be proud of?

I definitely didn't want to die in prison. I knew that as long as I didn't pick up a new charge in prison, kill someone or get killed that I would get out someday. Although that day was so far into the future that it was hard to envision, I knew that it existed.

I was aware, too, of the challenges I would face upon my release. I knew that I would not have any marketable job skills and that the likelihood of returning to prison was extremely high. How would I survive? How could I become successful? It just all seemed so hopeless.

Although it was very difficult, I came to believe that a better life was possible. I realized when I was around 20 and going into my third year in prison that the greatest resource that I would have when I was released was my mind.

Understanding that reality I decided that my best option would be to invest my time into developing my mind and my character. I began to educate myself. I read hundreds of books and learned how to meditate. I challenged myself and all that I had come to believe. I was setting out on a new path.

I tried to forget that I almost killed two people. I tried to forget all of the pain that I had brought into so many lives. I was struggling to become a better person, struggling to believe that to get out of prison and become successful without going back into a life of crime was possible. I didn't want to hurt people anymore because that is not who I am.

Yes, it is what I had become, but it wasn't and isn't who I am at my core. I looked around my environment for evidence that it was possible to change and succeed without going back into a life of crime and found none. I saw the same faces disappear and reappear year after year in that revolving door or recidivism. I found misery, negativity and hopelessness. Everyone was angry, frustrated and trying to answer the same fundamental question: What did I do to my life?

No one wakes up one morning and decides that they want to go to prison. And not many people in their childhood have dreams of becoming drug-dealing thugs. Most of us urban folks are just trying to survive and cope with the realities of inner city life the best way we can.

When I searched for strength within myself, I found only the smallest glimmer of hope. I held on to that small spark for dear life and often for my own sanity. It was just so difficult to believe that I could build a new life, but the alternative was completely unacceptable.

To not believe, to not imagine, to not attempt to visualize, even as an intellectual exercise to entertain myself, was akin to not living at all. To not believe meant accepting that my life, my entire existence, would be prison. To not believe meant that I would never have an opportunity to truly experience life again beyond those walls.

My situation was serious. When I attempted to imagine my life after prison, I kept coming up blank. I was deeply afraid of my future and the challenges I would face. I had yet to completely rule out returning to a life of crime. The dominant question that plagued my thoughts was, would the mistakes of my past prevent a better future? Could I rebuild my life after a major setback, or was I forever confined by these decisions?

## Today: Back on Track

After about twelve years in prison I looked around one day at my peers and realized that I had changed. I did it. I had finally freed myself from the mindset that led me there. I had finally learned to love myself and to believe in myself. But still I wondered, was it possible, after all the mistakes and bad decisions, for a person like me to reposition my life for success when I left the prison walls behind?

It's been almost five years since my release, and I can tell you that the answer is yes! I know this based on my own experience and am confident that anyone with a burning desire to be better and do better can overcome their mistakes and forge a path that will lead to a better quality life. In this book I will share with you some of the process that I developed to free myself from myself and reposition my own life for success. I come with one clearly defined message: *Your past does not have to determine your future.*

As you read, remember:

- I was a barely literate high school drop out with more issues than I could handle. I was lost somewhere deep within myself and trying to figure out how to escape from all of the pain and disappointment.

- I had no idea who I was and was desperately trying to be someone I thought would fit in and be accepted. I didn't like myself and had no idea that I hated myself. I couldn't love myself because I didn't know how.

- Everywhere I turned in those days I seemed to be reminded that I was worth less than others. I couldn't understand why the neighborhood thugs decided to bully me. These were guys I had grown up with.

- I lived in constant fear every time that I left out of the house. I took the longest routes whenever I could in an effort to avoid everyone.

- Finally, I became what I feared. I began making decisions that not only hurt myself but others as well. Drugs, guns, crime, prison.

These days, when I review my history, it seems like I'm looking at a stranger. It has taken me a considerable amount of time but I have indeed gotten my life back on track. It took me all of ten years to break free from the mindset that led me on a dangerous, destructive path. It was perhaps another two years before I truly believed that I could succeed without going back into a life of crime.

There were days in my cell when I tried to imagine what it would be like to hang myself. I have battled doubt and fear. I couldn't see a brighter future, only a darker one, determined by a past that would confine me to living a life of crime and prison.

It is now 2015 and I have been home for over four years. I am completely out of the corrections system and have my life back. When I got out, I had nothing but a vision for building a successful educational company based on the concept of "Empowerment through self-examination and personal responsibility that in grounded in real life experience. In addition to that vision, faith that it was possible to realize that vision and a commitment to do the work needed to make it happen.

It was that faith in what was possible that allowed me to find the strength to humble myself and do the things I needed to do to avoid going back into a life of crime. I applied for food stamps. I walked everywhere, I stayed with my mom and visited my father.

At the age of 34 it was easy to fall victim to comparing myself to others and feel insecure and worthless because I was less accomplished. At a time when most grown people are living on their own I am still not living on my own. Pride could have driven me insane and back to prison.

All of my clothes were some form of hand-me-down, but that was ok. I was free in mind, body and spirit. I went to business classes and rode the bus when I could. My brother gave me an old laptop computer to type on, and I used the internet at the library. In prison I fell in love with books and now I am a regular library visitor.

I had a TracFone with 250 minutes a month on it for communication. I had offers to sell a lot of drugs, but I refused. My mentor helped to get me a job, and I eventually got my first driver's license and my first car. It's not much but it's mine. I then began upgrading my phone and recently entered the world of the IPhone.

In the midst of putting my life back together I have continued to work on writing books, my business concept and plan. I have been blessed to meet some extremely wonderful people that have helped me along the way and have just begun attending community college. I plan to get a four-year degree in Entrepreneurship and perhaps beyond.

My life is a living testimony that profound change is indeed possible.

# 2    Choosing to Do Better

We all make decisions and engage in behavior that we aren't proud of or wish we could undo. Sometimes our intentions are good; sometimes not. Often the outcome is not what we anticipated.

All of us also have personal issues or problems that influence our decisions and actions. These issues vary from person to person and can have both positive and negative impact on our decision-making and on the paths we follow.

When our decisions or actions result in serious damage to ourselves or others, it's easy to think that because we cannot change what has happened, we cannot change. I have learned nothing is further from the truth *if we truly want to change*.

It has taken me some time to be able to express what I talk about in this book. I don't have anything original to say, just some life lessons that I have validated through my own experience and that I think can be useful to others who have found themselves in situations similar to those I experienced.

## Learning from the Past

It takes some of us longer than others to learn these lessons. There are those who when told not to stick their hands into a fire because it will burn them, listen and obey. Others hear but ignore the warning. I am one who heard and disobeyed; I had to get burned before I understood.

Most of us come to understand that we have been choosing to stick our hands into the fire. Then we realize that we can also choose to not stick our hands into that fire. Or, simply put, we get tired of being in situations that hurt us.

Of course, not all bad decisions and behavior lead to a prison cell. Some of you reading this book may have made mistakes in your marriage, done and said things that hurt your relationship beyond repair. You may not have always made the best decisions in raising your children. You could have spent more time with them, been a better role model, shown them more love. You may have made bad decisions with your credit, in your business, or with friendships.

You may have made decisions that led to alcohol, drugs and prison. You may have dropped out of school or become a parent when you were too young for that responsibility. Never forget, however, that you are not alone; we all have pasts and we all have made mistakes.

Fortunately, life is a process of growth and development, and our past experiences can lead to self-improvement and a better life. Just because we cannot change the past does not mean we cannot control our choices in the present and redirect our futures.

Too often we fall victim to a mindset that says that because of our past decisions we cannot do better and be better, that because of our past decisions we are somehow relegated and restricted to certain roles and paths, and that our fates have been sealed. This mindset becomes true *only if you choose to accept it as true*.

This means that failure to be a good husband or wife at some time in the past does not mean you can never build a successful marriage. Past failure to be a responsible mother or father does not mean you cannot become a good parent. And if your life has long been ruled by drug or alcohol addiction, it does not mean you cannot achieve lasting sobriety.

## The Incarcerated Mind

Physical chains are placed on a person to restrict movement. Psychological chains restrict the mind and can prevent us from directing our thoughts in a manner that allows us to move beyond past mistakes and build a better life. I think of this an "incarcerated mind."

With your mind in this state, your thinking is limited by beliefs or perceptions that cause you to continue to respond to your problems as you always have and result in similar outcomes. For example, perhaps you know a woman who is tired of being with men who don't respect and appreciate her, and yet she keeps choosing the same type of man. Different face, different body but each one brings the same problems and pain into her life.

Some would have us believe we have little or no power over our vices and lower desires and that we cannot overcome our weaknesses and be better and do better. This is true only if you choose to accept it as a truth for yourself. The moment you begin to reject this nonsense is the moment you can begin to take charge of your peace and happiness.

## The Influence of Outside Voices

Often it is easy to get caught up in other people's opinions of who we are and their judgments of our actions. We accept their labels and define ourselves according to mistakes we have made. But sometimes we can care too much about what others think of us, and that can affect our thinking and hinder our efforts to improve ourselves and our lives.

On the other hand, we can learn from others—those alive today and those who living before our time—from their trials, errors, challenges, failures and successes. I'm talking about folks who are battle tested. Folks who faced difficult challenges and have made some bad decisions because they had yet to acquire the tools needed to help them solve their problems in a positive way.

I am talking about people who despite being knocked down, got back up. People that have been through their own personal hell and survived. In a perfect world we wouldn't have to struggle and fall down, but this is not a perfect world and we are not perfect. Nevertheless, each of us has the innate ability to be better and do better.

### Renewing Your Mind

When have we not had the equal capacity to be an angel to one and a devil to another? When have we not have the equal ability to build and destroy? Each of us carries the seeds of good and evil within us. That is simply who we are as human beings—not some of us but all of us.

When we delude ourselves into believing otherwise, we become lost. Lost in our own ignorance of who and we are and are not. I believe in the possibility of transformation and that, as the apostle Paul said, transformation begins with the renewal of your mind.

It happens with a change in thinking. The idea is to replace your old ways of thinking with better ones. When your mind is renewed, you can begin acting differently and getting different results.

Transformation is an internal process. It doesn't have anything to do with anyone else.

Despite the fact that many people are trying to sell folks on quick fixes and overnight solutions, the truth is that transforming a life is not easy or quick, but it is possible.

That in essence is what this book is all about. That despite our past we can be better and do better.

# 3    How Did I Get into This Mess?

Have you ever asked yourself, how did I get into this mess? How can I prevent this from happening again? You keeping thinking about the situation and how it wasn't supposed to be like this.

If you can better understand how you got into the situation, then you can better position yourself to overcome and move past it. Here is what happened to me.

Because I was 17 on the night my crime was committed, I was sent to the New Castle County Juvenile Detention Center. In addition, it was my first time being detained, so I was allowed to stay at the center until my 19th birthday.

I spent 11 months there in a state of shock, unsuccessfully trying to understand how I had gotten into this mess of prison and facing a very bleak future. Being locked up was no longer something I saw in the movies or heard the guys in the neighborhood talk about.

## Denial

Everything felt so unreal to me, and I had yet to understand the seriousness of my situation. I kept hoping and often praying that it was all a dream. In those early days the only way that I could make sense of my situation was to become a victim and blame everyone for my decisions.

Was I wrong to want peace, happiness and success? Was I wrong to not want to live in constant fear of being humiliated, bullied to my emotional breaking point and beaten up? Was I wrong to start standing up for myself and taking my respect?

How was any of this my fault? What choice did I have? If my intended victim had not acted like he had a gun, I would not have fired my gun.

If he would not have challenged me, I would not be here. If he would have given my friend the drug money he owed, I would be free.

What about the guy I accidently shot in the chest? Well, I couldn't allow myself to think about that, so I pushed it to the back of my mind, pretending it didn't happen. But it did happen, and it was real.

When I was going to court to see if I would be tried as an adult, the victim's family came to testify about what happened. They said they were sitting at the kitchen table, heard a bang and then my victim fell over. They were so afraid he would die, and for what? What exactly did he do to deserve this? The young man sat in a wheelchair and explained to the court how difficult his life had become. He couldn't stand or sit for long periods.

His brothers glared at me from across the room, and I wondered why. I mean, I was there in the courtroom, but this wasn't me they were talking about—*it couldn't be*. They wished only the worst for me. I sat in silence listening to my victim speak from his wheelchair and thought, "This is bullshit; he's not that hurt." I became angry, very angry.

This wasn't the time for me to become soft-hearted and feel bad. I had to push those feelings to the deepest corner of my mind. It was just too much to deal with. I simply could not allow myself to feel the pain and guilt from what I had done.

## Reality

As the months passed and it became clear that I was going to be tried as an adult, and the worse my situation began to look. I kept thinking how none of this was part of the plan, and yet it had become my reality. I was facing between 36 and 72 years if I went to trial and lost. I was soon convinced that losing was almost destined.

How did I get myself into this mess was the question that haunted me, followed by how can I get out of it. In those days I was hopeful that the court would show some degree of leniency, but that didn't happen so my reality became a plea agreement to 18 years in prison.

At this point, although still in shock, I recognized that I had another opportunity at life, as far away as it was. I also began to understand that if I was to get my life back on track and prevent this from happening again, that I had to figure it out...how did I get into this mess?

# 4 Mindset, Decisions and Outcomes (MDO)

Mindset, Decisions and Outcomes, or MDO, are three elements of a framework that can help us better understand how our decisions and actions may have created an unexpected or undesirable outcome. Understanding the process that led to a setback can provide insight to help us move forward with our lives.

We can also use this framework to help us make better decisions in the future and minimize the risk of avoidable setbacks. This requires that we focus our attention on the outcome we would like to see and build a mindset that supports that outcome and guides our response to solving a problem or fulfilling a need.

In summary:

- A problem or need arises.
- Our belief system, or **mindset**, will influence our approach and options.
- Finally, we make a **decision** and take action.
- The **outcome** can be positive or produce negative, producing unintended consequences.

Here is how I applied this process in my life.

## The Problem

The problem I was trying to solve before my incarceration was to meet my basic survival needs. I was homeless, hungry and poorly clothed. I didn't know how long I would be able to stay at my friend's aunt's home or what would happen afterwards.

I was also extremely frustrated with the conditions of my life. The problems were real and calling for immediate attention. Something had to be done or I would face another night of uncertainly, another night of not knowing if and when I would eat.

The more I thought about it, I could only come up with one possible solution. I needed money and I needed it right away. Money would buy food, a motel room and the weed and alcohol I used to help me cope with life.

So how would I get this money? This is where mindset begins to play a major role in all of the events that were to follow. So what was my mindset?

**The Mindset**

After I dropped out of school, I started spending more time with my little crew of fellow outcasts within the housing projects. We were not the "cool" kids nor were we in the "A" crowd. There were about six of us, but my two best friends at the time were Hagz and Croft.

I had known Hagz for as long as I could remember. We were neighbors as small children. I met Croft when I was about 14 through Hagz, and we immediately clicked. Both of them had very difficult lives.

The streets were all they had. Both grew up with parents addicted to crack cocaine and alcohol. Life had not been kind to either one of them. I don't remember if Hagz ever made it to high school but Croft, the others and I did.

We didn't last long because we were often fighting, getting suspended and generally acting out. I think I may have been the last of our group to drop out. Croft had more pressing issues to deal with at the time, including being father to a young child, another on the way and his drug-addicted parents.

I never really thought about how much those things affected Croft and who he was. I never thought about how he actually felt about all of it. He, like Hagz, was dealing the best way he knew how: crime, drugs and violence.

So when I started spending more time with this group, I was exposed to the darker side of life. It was during this period that the mindset, which would ultimately lead me to spending more than 16 years in prison, began to form. At the time I had no understanding or awareness of what a mindset was, why it was important or how it impacts the way we experience life.

Like many of my friends, I also had no understanding of how powerful the human mind can be. I had no idea of how personal belief systems were built, maintained and destroyed. No one ever taught us those things in the hood. In fact, it took me years of study, meditation and reflection to begin to understand these things.

As a result, I had adopted a mindset of crime and violence, so when I had to solve the problem I described above, my solution was to rob someone. How else was I going to get money? Get a job? That was unlikely. Surely there were other options, you might argue. Well, yes and no.

On one level it is true that we all make choices and are responsible for the choices we make. I could have tried a number of things such as shelters, soup kitchens, reaching out to other people, going to a church for help, etc. All of that is true.

But what I have come to understand is that people are often limited by their beliefs and mindset. For example, although going to a church for help was an option, it was not one that existed in my mind. Therefore, it was not a choice for me. So I had to choose from the options that existed within my mind at the time, which were crime and violence.

## The Decision

With a mindset built on the belief that violence and crime were the most effective ways to solve my problems, I decided on armed robbery.

What happened? What were the outcomes I produced as a result?

Did I solve my problem? Did I accomplish my goal of improving my living conditions? Or did I create more problems for myself and further complicate my life?

## The Outcome

Not only did I fail to solve my problem and improve my living conditions, I also managed to create even more problems for myself.

My original problems of basic living and survival were for the most part limited to myself. My new problems not only complicated my own life but also the lives of others in ways I couldn't imagine when I woke up on the morning of July 10, 1995. As my life hung in limbo at the detention center, others were suffering also. Who else was impacted?

- The young man that I accidently shot and his family.
- The man I was trying to kill, his family and his girlfriend.
- My own family.
- Croft, who was with me, and his family.
- My girlfriend's family.
- My community and all of the people who were out the night that it happened and many more.

Although it took me a very long time to admit and accept the full impact of my decision, I am strong enough to do so today.

# 5  Mistakes and Bad Decisions

How can we move forward with our lives after experiencing a personal setback caused by mistakes and bad decisions? In answering this question, I want to begin with several definitions.

## Hindsight

Hindsight is being able to look at a situation after it has occurred and recognize where we went wrong. It involves understanding where and why we should have made different choices. The lessons of this book were derived from hindsight.

The ability to utilize hindsight is a very important skill in helping us minimize the number of mistakes we make. The problem with hindsight is that it takes place after the fact, after we have made a bad choice and complicated our lives .That is why we need another tool called foresight.

## Foresight

Foresight is the ability to look into the future and see what might happen. There is nothing mystical about this. The process for doing this is called *visualization*. The ability to visualize something in your mind is a part of that divine power that lies within each of us.

Understanding hindsight and foresight are important because you have to be able to learn from your mistakes and then use what you learned to make better choices.

## What Is a Mistake?

For the purpose of this book we will define a mistake as *a choice you make that produces negative and unwanted consequences that make your life more difficult.*

Note that the first part of the definition places the power to improve the conditions of your life in your hands. It says, a *choice you make*. This definition reflects a point of view that says you have *options* when you make a decision or take action. Here is where your true power is: you are not a helpless victim in life. You have choices about what's going on in your life'; you can stand up to yourself and for yourself.

When determining if a decision was right or wrong, you should consider the following question: Did your decision bring you closer to your goal or push you further away? If it brought you closer to your goal, it may be viewed as the right one. If it pushed you away, it may be viewed as wrong.

While the first part of our definition points to the inner world of power and causes, the second part speaks to the outer world of effects and consequences. It says *that produces negative and unwanted consequences that make your life more difficult.*

This wording suggests a connection between your unhappiness and your thinking. *Negative and unwanted* means you are not happy and at peace with the result of your decision or action. It may also mean that you have created more problems.

What is the difference between a bad decision and a good decision? Well it depends. In my experience I have found that the best way to determine the difference depends on what it is that you want or your goal.

A bad decision moves you away from accomplishing your desired outcome and produces unintended outcomes that negatively impact your life. A good decision moves you closer to accomplishing your goals.

These are very simple definitions but embodied within them is a way to look at and measure our decisions prior to making them. In addition to that we can also use this to help us get back on track if we should happen to lose sight of what our goals are.

In summary, you can save yourself a lot of pain and suffering by:

- using hindsight to examine the outcomes of your decisions and actions;

- recognizing a bad decision or mistake, that is, one that has not solved your problem or has created new ones; and

- Applying foresight to help you make better choices as you move ahead.

- Good decisions move use closer to our goals and bad decisions move use further away.

## Why Do We Make Mistakes?

While I was trying to figure out how I was going to put my life back together, I kept asking myself why I made the decisions and took the action I did. Because my outcome resulted in such a long prison sentence, I had a lot of time—*years*—to think and reflect.

I knew that if I did not at least develop a framework for understanding why I did what I did, it could happen again. The probability I would return to prison was high. All of the odds were stacked against me: I was young, uneducated, and barely literate with some serious issues.

In my heart I was determined to defeat the odds, *no matter what it took*. I knew things had to change in my life but I did not know what or how to do it. What I did understand was that if I did not figure it out, I would be back in prison one day and might not leave alive.

Here are five factors that contributed significantly to the terrible decisions I made in July 1995:

1. **Ignorance.** By ignorance I mean the following: not knowing how to get what you want without hurting yourself and making your life more complicated and difficult; not

understanding why you want something, what it represents to you, what need or desire or void it fulfills; and not realizing that you have options and the ability to make a choice.

2. **Wrong mindset.** I mentioned mindset earlier. If you have a mistaken perception of a situation or if the way you choose to look at it is flawed, then your thinking—*about how to get what you want and why*—is wrong. What you are feeding your mind will not produce the result you want. You will be jumping to conclusions without having all the facts, looking at the situation as you want or imagine it to be instead of is the way it really is.

3. **Lack of self-control.** Many bad decisions result from a lack of self-control. When your impulses and desires overpower your ability to think things through—and weigh the possible consequences of a decision or action—you run the risk of making poor, even life-altering, decisions.

4. **Emotional instability**. When you allow emotions such as sadness, anger, disappointment and fear to cloud your judgment and control your decisions, the result can be impulsive and harmful behavior. Situations such as the one I was in during the summer of 1995 produce stresses that can trigger the negative emotions that can get you into trouble. Fortunately, you can learn to cope with stress and manage your emotional health through sharing your concerns and emotions, thinking before you make a decision or take action and, if needed, seeking professional help.

# 6  A Foundation for Change

How do you begin the process of moving forward with your life after a personal setback caused by bad decisions?

- You have to want better for yourself.

- You have to define what better means to you.

- You have to imagine or visualize a better life.

- You must believe that better is possible.

- You have to find examples for inspiration.

- You have to commit to making better happen.

**Want Better for Yourself**

*Enough is enough.* In order for any type of change to occur within your life you have to reach a point where enough is simply enough. You have to reach this point from somewhere deep inside of you; you must make a commitment to change; mere words will not make it so.

When you reach this point of knowing that change has to occur—I mean *really knowing it*—then the process can begin. Change can be scary because of the fear of the unknown, but do not allow fear to prevent you from moving forward. You know what "the same" looks and feels like. You have to keep in mind all of the reasons why enough is enough. What are you sick and tired of? Why do you want something different?

If you choose to give into fear, there will not be any change or improvement in your life. What is important to remember is that *you do not have to make changes all at once*. You can and should take small steps. Taking small yet focused steps towards your goal can help you cope with the fear.

**Define What Better Means to You**

Begin the process of determining what better means to you by answering the following questions: What's wrong with now? What are the problems you are facing and how did they come about?

Next, think about what you want in a better life. Ask yourself what you want to eliminate, what you want to improve and what to add.

For example, you may want to eliminate living day to day or dependence on drugs or alcohol or engaging in criminal behaviors; you may want to live in a better neighborhood, improve relationships with family or get better job skills; or you may want to finish high school or go to college or get a car.

After you determine what will make your life better, ask yourself how and why these changes will improve your life.

**Imagine or Visualize a Better Life**

Imagination, or visualization, is a powerful tool that can be used to help you move toward the better you have defined. We use this tool when we find ourselves daydreaming and fantasizing about things we wish for. Haven't you pictured yourself living the life of the rich and famous or owning a shiny new car or hanging out with a favorite celebrity?

When it comes to visualizing your better life, you should engage your imagination with intent, purpose, determination and the faith that better is possible. So instead of random daydreaming, you should focus on images of your better life.

For example, let's say you are looking for a partner for a serious relationship. To visualize the kind of person you want to find, you would ask yourself what qualities are important to you: age, appearance, education, values and beliefs, family relationships, stability, kindness, sense of humor, interests, and so on. This would help you create pictures in your in your mind and perhaps recall some people you already know.

# A View of
# Better

*I wanted better for myself than to die in prison. I wanted to succeed, to achieve the American dream. I wanted to be happy, at peace within myself and successful. I wanted my life back.*

*I wanted some simple pleasures, small things. Things like having a room to myself and being able to take a shower when I wanted to. Things like having people in my life and sharing my space with people I actually liked, people I chose to be a part of my life and who weren't forced upon me.*

*I wanted the freedom of being able to come and go as I pleased.*

*Better for me meant having more options. Options like having my books and going to the library to continue my education. Better for me meant not being forced to deal with correctional officers who failed to acknowledge me as a human being.*

*Better for me meant dying with a clear conscience knowing that I had strived to right my wrongs by helping more people that I hurt. Better for me meant no longer hating myself but honestly loving who I am.*

## Believe That Better Is Possible

*Belief inspires action.* After you have decided that enough is enough and you want better for yourself than your current situation, you have to believe that change is possible. Belief inspires action, and action leads to results. If you do not believe that it is possible for you to achieve your goals, it is unlikely you will take the steps that are needed to do so.

While believing is often easier said than done, you can begin with having what Napoleon Hill in his book, *Think and Grow Rich*, called *having a burning desire*. This provides the fuel to get you started. Then keep reminding yourself of why you want better than your current situation. This will further fuel your desire. One of the most important lessons I have learned is the power of beliefs and what we are capable of achieving when we believe in something. It is our belief that something is possible that inspires us to take action.

If you do not believe that you can achieve a goal or make a change in your life, it is unlikely you will even try. For example, I definitely do not believe that I can become a professional basketball player. Since I do not believe this is possible for me, attempting to do so would be a waste of time. I do believe, however, that I can become a successful entrepreneur, and that belief inspires me to take action.

It certainly did not begin like this. Believing that I could successfully move forward with my life was perhaps one of my greatest challenges.

After I was sentenced to 18 years in prison, I had no idea what I was going to do with my life. I knew I wanted to be successful but I also knew it was unlikely that I would leave prison with any marketable jobs skills or enough education to succeed even if I did get a job. Although I was in prison, I still desired a piece of the American Dream.

I hoped that one day I would own a home of my own and have all I needed and most of what I wanted. But this was, for the most part, wishful thinking and a way for me to escape from the cell. My body may have been trapped in that cell, but my mind was free to come and go as it pleased.

Then I read the book *Rich Dad, Poor Dad* by Robert T. Kiyosaki. This book is considered by many to be one of the best personal finance books ever written. In the book Kiyosaki expresses a simple idea that completely changed how I looked at my situation.

That idea is that instead of saying that you *cannot* afford something, you should begin to ask yourself *how you could afford it*. I then began to ask myself how I could succeed in spite of my past.

My answer was entrepreneurship. Like most people I know that have been in the drug business, ownership is a natural inclination. We were already groomed with the principles of self-employment and being your own boss. I started to brainstorm and imagine myself owning businesses and running companies. I began to believe in my visions. But that's only part of it.

The next part was crucial: I had to become a *seeker*. I had no idea how to go from vision to reality, but I was determined to find out. That is what being a seeker is about. I read Kiyosaki's next book, a few that he recommended and then others I discovered on my own. What I found through reading reinforced my belief and gave me confidence to keep going.

### Find Examples to Inspire You

One of the best ways you can build confidence is to find examples of people who have faced and overcome similar or more difficult challenges in life. You can draw on these examples for inspiration and they become evidence of what is possible.

I was in my tenth or eleventh year in prison when I began to realize the importance of this. At the time I was completing a long-term drug treatment program and was required to do a presentation to graduate. I was unsure of what to speak about until I came across a magazine article that became my proof.

I don't remember if the article was in *Essence* or *Black Enterprise* magazine, but it was about ex-offenders who became successful entrepreneurs. The article profiled several people, all of whom had spent more than five years in prison. One became a successful publisher of urban fiction; another was a self-published author of urban fiction who sold tens of thousands of books in New York City out of his van; and another learned to cook in prison and became a chef.

Here was proof that my terrible decisions and the prison term that followed did not have to determine my future.

## Commit to Making Better Happen

Once you have determined what better is for you and why, you must commit to making it happen. Keep in mind that you do not need to have all the answers, but two prerequisites are key:

1. You must be willing to confront yourself with honesty.

2. You must be willing to accept yourself and what you discover.

In order to create the better life you envision, you must be willing to acknowledge the person you are and to take responsibility for your choices and the outcomes they have produced. This step is about honest self-examination. You can do this privately or you may choose to share your thoughts with someone if that will help.

It takes courage to honest with yourself about yourself, but the purpose is not to beat yourself up over choices that you have made. The purpose is to acknowledge that you are in control and have the ability to make changes in your life that will lead to a better future.

What are some of the areas in your life that you should examine?

- Your strengths and weaknesses or limitations

- Your wants and fears; likes and dislikes

- The kind of person you want to be

- Negative and positive influences in your life

- Choices you have made, the reasoning behind them and the outcomes

- The changes you will need to make if you want a better life

Be willing to accept what you discover about yourself. It's OK if you don't like what you see; we all experience those moments. What is important to keep in mind is that *you can choose to be better and do better*.


**You Are Not Your Mistakes**

If you were to buy into the one-sided portrayal often presented in the media or by others of people like me, you might conclude that there is no good in us. Why else would we knowingly choose to do many of the violent and self-destructive things we do?

Looking at individuals and situations through such narrow lenses can lead to incomplete perceptions of people and actions. There is no denying I have done my share of wrong things, but that doesn't mean I am without conscience.

I used to wonder what kind of person I was. Some people saw the good in me, many saw the bad and some saw both. I didn't know what to think. I didn't feel like a bad person nor did I think of myself as such. But I knew all of the things I had done, all of the people I had hurt.

I spent years ignoring what happened because to face it would have been too much. I spent years placing blame on others in an effort to justify my decisions because to take responsibility was too painful. I was defining myself according to my mistakes and struggling to believe that I was worth anything.

In the mist of all of this there was something in me that kept pushing me to improve myself. It was only recently, while working on this book, that I remembered what it was.

## A Seed Was Planted

When I was in the juvenile detention center, most of the staff and teachers took a liking to me. But there was one who looked into the eyes of the 18-year-old me and saw the man I was to become. Her name is Rose Wooten, and she is responsible for planting a seed that said that I could be more than what I was, that I could be better and do better.

Every day in class she gave us little one-page stories of great African-Americans. Who would have guessed that reading those little papers would give me the courage to read and ultimately summon that little piece of Divine within me to rise to the top?

I wasn't even aware that she was planting seeds. She saw a human being first and what I had done second. She had kindness, love and compassion in her eyes when she looked at me. She didn't see an animal; she saw what could have been her own child. And she saw this while fighting cancer and struggling through chemotherapy.

And then there was Reverend Aaron Moore who prayed with me at the detention and adult correction centers.

**You Versus Your Mistakes**

Your mistakes do *not* have to define who you are and what you are capable of unless you allow them to. Always remember:

- You can choose to be better and do better.

- You can learn from your experiences and use them to help you to make better decisions.

- You control your decisions and how you respond—mentally, emotionally and physically—to the situations presented to you.

**Dealing with the Outcomes of a Mistake**

When you realize you have made a bad decision or mistake, focus on the solution. If you visualize or imagine the possibilities, it will help to give you confidence and hope that you can make a comeback.

Do not focus on the problem and all of the things that you have done wrong. This will paralyze you, and you will be stuck in your past. *As long as you remain in the past you cannot move forward*. Also, when you focus on the mistakes you have made, you can start to feel really bad and helpless to be better and do better.

It is OK to feel hurt, disappointed and even angry. These are natural emotions, and we all have to deal with them, but you do not want to let your emotions cloud your perception of who you can be.

So you made a bad decision. You can still choose to be better and do better. The key is to make a decision is to dust yourself off, as the saying goes, and start again.

Ask yourself what was the lesson you were supposed to learn from the situation. Many times, if we look carefully and honestly at the problems we have created for ourselves, we will see that they can be viewed as blessings in disguise.

What I mean is that very often these situations will reveal to us the weaknesses we need to work on. So ask yourself what your situation reveals to you about yourself. What steps or changes in thinking or behavior can you make to avoid the type of difficulties you are in?

# 7   Preparing for Change

You have two options after you have made a mistake or bad decision: You can wallow in the mess you have created or you can do something about it.

It is acceptable to feel bad, be angry or cry. You can also pray, meditate and reflect, but after that, *what are you going to do?* I am assuming that you have made it this far in this book because you are determined to move toward being better and doing better.

### Change Your Point of View

You can turn your mistakes and bad decisions into life lessons. Start by changing your point of view so you are in a positive mindset. Realize that there is a lesson in this experience that will help you become a stronger and better person. Then make it your mission to find out what that lesson is.

### Analyze and Extract

To analyze your situation, find time to be alone with your thoughts. You do not want to be distracted from your mission. Once you are alone with your thoughts, just breathe and let thoughts flow.

First, use this time to think about your life and what you want it to be. Do not focus on your mistakes and how they complicated your life.

Next, visualize or relive the decision or action that led to an undesirable outcome. Try to be objective and hold off your emotions. This means that you should view the situation as though you were someone else. As you relive it, consider what you could have done. Imagine what would have happened if you had made different decisions.

To truly get to the root cause of your situation, keep asking yourself why something happened. For example, let's say you were mad. Ask yourself why you were mad. If your answer is that you felt disrespected or hurt, ask why you felt this way. If was because someone was ignoring what you said, again, ask why.

The more difficult part of exercise is to put yourself in the other person's shoes. I mean to really imagine that you are the other person. Using the example above, try to determine why the person ignored you—from his or her point of view.

To summarize:

- Find a quiet place and clear your mind.

- Think about the life you want, not your mistakes.

- Visualize the action that led to an undesired outcome. Consider what might have happened if you had made other decisions.

- Ask yourself why you did what you did.

- If your actions were triggered by other individuals, try to put yourself in their positions or minds.

Now you are ready to determine what you have learned from your experience and how can you use what you have learned to make better choices.

# 8 Keys to Success

## Acknowledge Your Role

For a long time I blamed my intended victim for the decision I made that sent me to prison. I used the excuse that I thought he had a gun and that I believed that if I pulled mine out, I had to use it.

The truth is that I provoked the entire situation. I am the one who started an argument with my intended victim's girlfriend, which led to my trying to kill him.

I saw her, disrespected her and tried to intimidate her. She stood up for herself. I then attempted to do the same with her boyfriend. Although money was involved and the situation was certainly not that simple, it remains true that I provoked the situation.

At the time I felt it was my duty to address the situation. I thought that although he owed my friend money, I would benefit from collecting it. *The truth is that I was not obligated to do anything.* In addition, had I not tried to intimidate her, it is quite possible that the entire situation would have been avoided.

When we take a look at mindsets and decisions, we realize that we make decisions using the options that our mindsets provide. My mindset at the time failed to offer many options. My choices seemed to be violence and crime.

Our mindsets will remain the same until we make the decision to elevate our thinking. When we begin to elevate our thinking, we become more aware and create more options to choose from. It took me at least three years to realize that I had had other options and I didn't have to fire the gun.

Reaching this realization complicated things even more because I had to begin the journey of moving out of the victim mentality. I was forced to acknowledge the role I played in the situation. Doing so created a real emotional crisis for me. I had to look at myself with honesty, acknowledge what I had become and question what type of person I truly wanted to be.

I could no longer hide behind the belief that none of this was my fault. There was no longer that psychological safety net. It was a very hard time but one that led to empowerment.

# Getting Honest
# with Myself

*The motives behind the event that sent me to prison began out of a sense of blind loyalty and self-defense but progressed into an issue of pride because my intended victim would not bow down to my then-perceived sense of authority: I had a loaded gun; I deserved respect.*

*While on the surface it was true that I initially thought my target had a gun when he reached into his waistline, after I pulled out my gun I saw he didn't.*

*After realizing there was no threat to my life, I still kept the gun aimed at him. When he decided to challenge me, I decided to kill him. I told myself for years it was because I accepted that if you pull a gun on someone, you have to use it.*

*That belief influenced my thinking and decision at the time. However, as I delved into my own mind and spirit, I realized that my true motive was pride. I didn't want to kill him because I felt physically threatened or because I believed I had to use the gun once I pulled it out. I tried to kill him because he threatened my perception and image of myself.*

*My personal transformation was from a soft-spoken and scared churc-going kid who was constantly made fun of and bullied into an outlaw who stood up for himself. I believed that the image I was projecting was intimidating and to be respected. As I stood there with a fully loaded, sawed- off shotgun aimed at my victim, I expected him to humble himself and cower in my presence.*

*I was a developing gangster, and it was his responsibility to respect that or face the consequences. When he looked at me and said, "Do what you gotta do," I felt beyond disrespected. For me, he wasn't just challenging me, to see if I had the courage to pull the trigger. He was challenging my very identity and existence.*

*He was attempting to send me back to those days of being humiliated, intimidated, chased home, beaten up by groups and living in constant fear. I was not going back to living like that. I didn't want much, just for people to leave me alone and let me live my life and mind my own business. I felt that was being threatened.*

**Accept**

After you have taken the time to look into the mirror and be honest with yourself, the next step is to accept what you have seen.

In time I came to accept that I was wrong on several levels, misguided and ignorant. I could have chosen to make different decision. Real people were hurt, lives changed and negatively impacted because of a decision that I made. No one forced me to do what I had done. There is no one for me to blame for my decision but myself.

Accepting this level of personal responsibility is, in my opinion, essential for growth and development. A huge side effect of the victim mindset is a feeling of helplessness. When we are able to take responsibility and say that we choose, we empower ourselves with the ability to do and be better.

I grew up in an environment where violence is taught as a primary method to resolve conflict. As a result of that upbringing, I slowly began to accept that as a way of life. It took more than a decade in prison before I began to understand that I could choose my beliefs.

In doing this I began to appreciate what it means to look into the mirror and accept responsibility for my decisions. Even more than that, I began to understand that I also had to accept responsibility for my education. I reasoned that if what I fed my mind led me to prison, than changing that mental diet would keep me out.

Acceptance is not about admitting anything to anyone but yourself. It is not about making some public announcement that you were wrong or anything like that. It is about accepting things in your own mind, heart and spirit and then taking responsibility to do something to be and do better.

## How to Move Forward: Six Steps

Once you make a decision to accept responsibility for the part you played in your problems, your role is to learn from it and become a better person.

**Step 1: Don't look back.** Do not be paralyzed by your mistakes and stuck in your past. Instead focus on your goals. Although the memories of our bad decisions and mistakes will remain with us, it is more profitable to spend our time trying to create solutions instead of dwelling on the problem.

The problem will not be solved just because we dwell on it, complain about it or beat ourselves up over it. The problem will be resolved and things will improve when we commit to doing something about it and then follow through with our solutions.

**Step 2: Forgive yourself.** It is easy to get caught up in believing and convincing yourself that you are a horrible person. Forgiving yourself means that, although you live with the pain, guilt and shame, you choose not to beat yourself up and belittle or put yourself down.

**Step 3: Raise the bar.** Elevate your thinking. Educate yourself. Know that the level of thinking that caused e problems in your life is not the same level of thinking that will

76

provide a solution and allow you to overcome the problem.

For example, if on a scale of one through ten, a level six mindset caused the problem in your life, then at the very least you need a level seven mindset to solve the problem. This means that you are going to have to fill your mind with new and different information and better ways of dealing with your issues than you previously used.

For example, I once terrorized a family because the husband owed me money for crack. The family had small children in their house, but in the middle of the night I kicked all of windows in and probably kicked at the door also.

A few days later his wife came to me with the majority of the money and said to please leave her family alone. She was all of five feet tall and the look in her eyes said she wasn't afraid of me. That moment hurt me so much, but I couldn't let anyone know that. I couldn't risk being looked at as being soft.

What I wanted was a stable place to live and a means to feed myself. Again I believed that the best way for me to get those things was criminal activity. All it got me was a long prison sentence.

I saw this time and time again while I was in prison: people caught up in the cycle of recidivism primarily as a result of not elevating their thinking, educating themselves in a constructive way and expanding the options that existed within their own minds.

I knew that the type of thinking that got me into that situation would not be the type of thinking I needed to get out. I had to step up my game. I had to educate myself about myself. It wasn't enough to know that I got angry and attempted to kill someone. I needed to know why I got angry. I needed to know why his words bothered me so much. I needed to know and understand my own weakness and insecurities so that I could work on improving them.

I had to educate myself about the power of my own mind. I had to find solutions and look within myself for answers to problems that were equally within me.

There will always be situations and circumstances beyond our individual control, but we always have it within our means and power to choose how we respond to those things.

***Step 4: Have greater expectations and standards for yourself.*** In the beginning I had very low, if any, expectations of myself. I just kept making bad decisions and trashing my life based on my own ignorance—ignorance in the truest sense of not knowing how to resolve my problems without hurting myself and others.

What did I expect of myself? I wasn't expected to respect or love myself so I didn't. These days my expectations are to maintain my own peace and happiness. These days I expect to honor the relationship that I have with the Source, or God if you will, and the path that I have been called to.

To say that I once had no standards would be an understatement. All that has changed. I now have standards in my relationships. Although I am not very judgmental—and with good reason—I don't allow anyone into my space. Without having personal standards any and everything will be in your life, bringing all types of nonsense and drama along.

I strive to keep people around me who want things out of life similar to what I want. These are positive, caring and good people.

***Step 5: Demand more and better for yourself and of yourself.*** These days I demand more and better of myself than dying in prison. I demand more and better of myself than ignorance. I demand improvement and education. I demand that I do the best I can while continuing to learn from my mistakes. I demand that I get back up every single time that I fall down and fight again.

I demand that I be a better child to my parents and a better member of my family. I demand that I be a better and more responsible member of the community, society and humanity.

***Step 6: Commit to being better and doing better.*** It is not enough to simply say that we demand more and better of ourselves. As I said earlier, we have to commit to being better and doing better. To commit to something means that we will not waver when times get hard and revert back to our old and ineffective ways of doing things.

When I go out of jail, I didn't own anything and had to use food stamps until I was able to get a job. This was extremely difficult for me because my plans were to have stable employment and save money while I worked on my business plans.

But things did not work out that way and the streets were calling me. Almost every week it seemed I had an opportunity to get back into the drug game. I refused—time and time again. I was battling with myself and my new image of myself.

I was feeling like a failure before I even started. I was in my mid-thirties, on welfare and living with my mom. Later on we started having a series of issues with the bills and facing eviction—the same situation that happened when I was 17.

I struggled with my definition of a man and my responsibility to my parents. What kind of man would I be to allow my mother to be in a shelter again? I was no longer a child. The streets called me again and with a much more lucrative opportunity.

I thought about it. Then I prayed and meditated on it. I was quite afraid at the time. I knew that type of person that I would have to become if I got back into the streets. I didn't want to be that person. I didn't want to hurt people anymore or go back to prison.

I thought about all of the people that I would be letting down who had come to believe in me, my message and my mission. I was afraid to have faith because faith requires that you trust and have confidence when there is no evidence of success to easy your doubts and fears.

I faced that same challenge of faith in prison, but this was different. I sat on my bed with my legs crossed, forearms resting on my knees and palms up, focusing on my breathing. About a half hour into my meditation I heard, *Be calm, stay the course. I spared you for a reason, you are here for a purpose. Stay the course, and you will have all that you desire.* I heard and I obeyed. I refused the offer and continued to struggle. My commitment to being better and doing better was not subject to change when difficult times were upon me.

# 9   The Challenges Ahead

## Managing Your History

You will still think about your mistakes and the consequences that followed but you will begin thinking about them less when you focus your attention on your new goals and your progress.

## Work in Progress

Remember that life is about growth and development, so you will continue to make mistakes and bad decisions. With practice, however, your decision-making will get better. Understand that you are a work in progress (as we all are), which means that you are not without flaws but you are working to improve yourself by investing in your mind and your character.

## Doubts and Fears

There will be times when you begin to doubt that it's possible for you to succeed; that's OK. There is a way to deal with these feelings. This is where investing in your mind comes into play. *To be very clear about investing, I mean that you will do the work necessary for you to succeed.*

As I said previously, when it comes to addressing your doubts one of the best things that you can do is to find examples of people who have faced challenges similar to yours and have managed to overcome them and succeed. This is feeding your mind the food it needs to make your vision of personal success a reality.

*There is no short cut or escaping the fact that you must do the work.* What this process will do for you is increase your confidence in yourself. As you grow more confident in what you are capable of, it becomes easier, as Nike says to "just do it."

This is not to say that change will be easy or quick, but if you stay focused and take small steps you will get there. Fear is also natural, but you can't allow your fear to prevent you from trying to be better and do better. What do you have to lose? You have already been through hell.


**What Others Think**

People will always have something to say about you, no matter what you are doing. Many will remember your mistakes and failures, make harsh judgments and place labels on you. That is simply a reality that happens to everyone at some time and that you will have to deal with. My advice to you on this is to ignore them.

If you spend a lot of time worrying about what people think of you, it will be extremely difficult for you to focus on your goals and move forward. I am not saying that some of the things that people may say about you will not hurt because they will. What you have to remember is that those who may criticize you are moving along with their lives, and you should, too.

What I do know is that if you actively work on becoming a better person and invest in your mind and character, there are people who will accept you. Not only will they accept you but they may be willing to help you because, believe it or not, they have also made mistakes and bad decisions, so they understand.

What they won't do is invest their time and energy in a person who wants something handed to them and is not willing to do the work.

That is perfectly understandable; no one has any time for that nonsense. Either you want it or you don't, and if you don't that's fine, but don't waste others' time. Come back when you are ready.

Lastly, I believe you should know that there will be a lot of people that won't accept you or be willing to help you. In fact, there are some people who will seemingly do everything in their power to make life difficult for you.

My advice here is twofold. One, you have to get in touch with that power within you that is greater than the challenges that you face. For many people this is found in their spirituality and religion. Let that be your anchor when times get rough. And two, I strongly suggest that you surround yourself with people who do believe in you.

### Labels
**Definitions belong to the definers, not the defined.**
Toni Morrison, *Beloved*

Just because someone chooses to label you based on your mistakes and bad decisions does not mean you have to accept it.

You have the power to define yourself however you see fit. Why not choose a positive label for yourself that inspires you to move forward despite the challenges that you face?

# 10   What It Means to Be Human

**"If you live long enough, you'll make mistakes. But if you learn from them, you'll be a better person. It's how you handle adversity, not how it affects you. The main thing is never quit, never quit, never quit".**

President William J. Clinton

I am not a religious person but I do consider myself to be deeply spiritual. I believe that something greater than my individual self is the cause of all that is in existence. We may not share the same views on what that something is, but throughout the world and the ages people sought, defined and followed through a variety of forms a higher power.

I don't often speak about my spirituality because I think that it's something personal and should be held close to one's heart. I believe and feel that I was spared because I am purposed. It has been faith and a deep connection and understanding with the Source that has guided me.

I am fortunate that no one died as a result of my decisions, but people could have. I could still be in prison serving a life sentence or, even worse, awaiting the death penalty. Instead I am here because something moved inside me that I didn't understand and guided me to this point in my life.

Clearly, I have not always made the best decisions. In fact, I have not always made even good decisions. I do not claim to be anything more than I am. I am a simple man who has been learning what it means to be human.

In my heart I choose to believe that all of my life's experiences were in preparation for this very time—a time for me to teach, guide and lead, to become, as we say, part of the solution. I cannot sit on the sidelines any more than I can control the blood running through my veins. My spirit demands otherwise

Something has guided me to where I am today. I have stood in the eye of the storm, been knocked down and broken, and then picked up and put back together. Humbled and grateful, I am living testimony of what is possible and what it means to be human.

I am humbled and grateful that I have received another opportunity. An opportunity that I still struggle with in terms of being worthy and deserving. I was once told that it was pure luck that spared me from having a life sentence or perhaps the death penalty.

For a long time I never knew what to make of some of the events that happened in my life. When I was at my lowest point and in my darkest moments—and all seemed lost and I was without hope—I sensed something moving in me that I could not understand or describe. It seemed as though I was being reminded of something I had forgotten, that I was supposed to be doing something but forgot what it was.

It wasn't until the end of my prison sentence that I finally realized that what I was feeling or sensing came from a source bigger than me, and I began to understand what my purpose is. I do not believe in coincidence. I was afforded this opportunity for a specific purpose and I am submitting to the will of that which brought me out and saw me through.

My struggles have not been in vain, so I am grateful that I have another chance to get it right—*another chance to be better and do better.*

I am standing on something today and I am standing in something. I am standing in the spirit of greatness. In the spirit of greatness that is within each of us. Greatness that has neither beginning nor ending. A greatness that I never knew existed until it moved in me.

There is a saying that circumstances will reveal a man to himself, meaning that we will learn who we are in the defining moments of life. I have learned who I am, so today I am standing up.

I believe in self-empowerment through self-examination and personal responsibility. There are a lot of things that we cannot change or control. I cannot change my history; what's done is done.

I cannot take that shot back and I cannot take back the pain I have caused or the blood I have shed. I cannot control how people feel about me. Some will love me and some will hate me, but I cannot control that either. It is what it is.

Some people will criticize, categorize, judge and look down their noses at me. That's cool because I cannot control that either so I'm not going to stress over it.

*What I can do is wake up each morning, put one foot in front of the other and strive to be the best person that I can be.* To continually work on improving myself and overcoming my weaknesses. To treat people with respect and kindness.

I can work to forgive as I have been forgiven, love as I have been loved and give compassion as I have received it. To do the best I can to be an example and guide to a generation that is severely lacking these things and in need of them.

Will I always succeed at this? Probably not because I am human and will continue to make mistakes. But one of my strongest held values is that I have a fundamental conviction that every human being has the capacity for growth and development. We can all be better and do better if we choose to do so.

So I encourage you to keep on fighting, to keep on standing up to yourself, to keep challenging and fighting yourself to become a better you. A friend of mine has a saying:

**My past is a place of *reference* and not a place of *residence*.**

I ask you to keep believing in yourself even if no one else does. I encourage you to love yourself even if no one else does and remember that you and you alone are responsible for your own inner peace and happiness.

Thank you for your support.

## Keys to Making Good Decisions

Know **1)** what you want, **2)** what you do *not* want, and **3)** why.

Determine what you have to do to **1)** get what you want, and **2)** avoid what you don't.

Consider the possible **outcomes**. Think things through.

Develop a plan that will not complicate your life or result in unintended consequences.

Stay focused.

Fight yourself. Do not allow your emotions to cloud your thinking.

Made in the USA
Las Vegas, NV
22 November 2021

35042994R00056